Twisters

Countdown!

Kay Woodward
and Ofra Amit

Evans

Countdown!

First published 2005
Evans Brothers Limited
2A Portman Mansions
Chiltern Street
London W1U 6NR

Text copyright © Evans Brothers Limited 2005
© in the illustrations Evans Brothers Limited 2005

British Library Cataloguing in Publication Data
Woodward, Kay
     Countdown!. – (Twisters)
     1. Children's stories – Pictorial works
     I. Title
     823.9'2 [J]

ISBN 0237529270
13-digit ISBN (from 1 January 2007) 9780237529277

Printed in China by WKT Company Limited

Series Editor: Nick Turpin
Design: Robert Walster
Production: Jenny Mulvanny
Series Consultant: Gill Matthews

It's time to go.

Ready for countdown.

Ten…

...a super-clean astronaut.

Nine…

...a shiny spacesuit.

Eight...

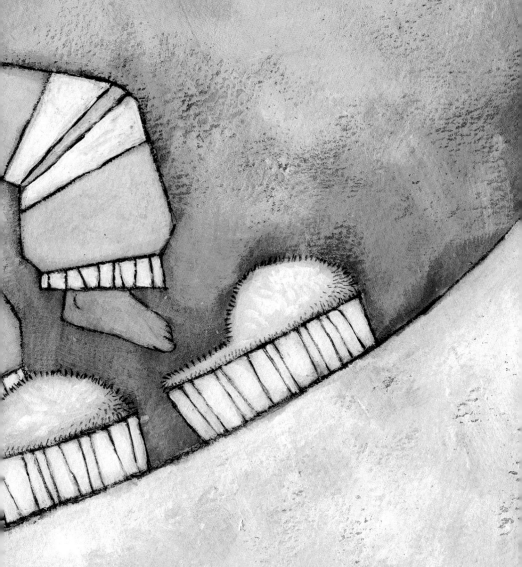

...moon shoes.

Seven…

...a rocket book.

Six…

…space juice.

Five...

...a clever co-pilot.

Four…

...a helmet.

Three...

...galactic goggles.

Two…

...a walkie-talkie.

One...

...here's my spaceship.

Zero…

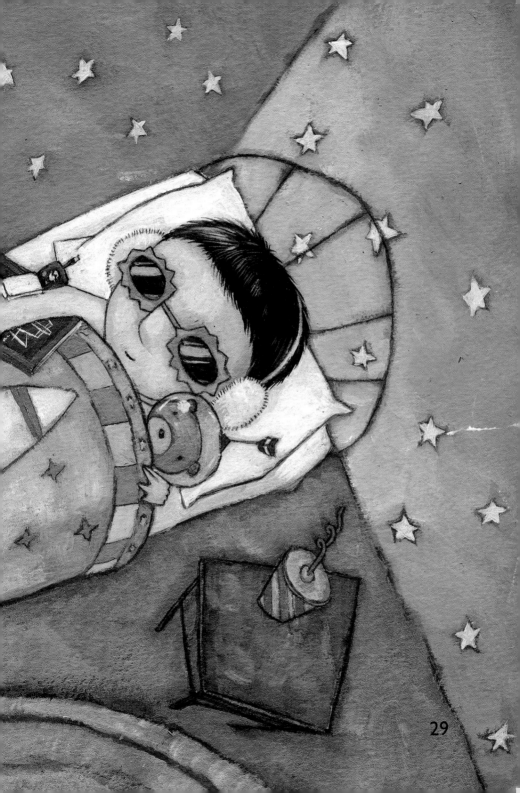

ZZZzzzzz!

Why not try reading another Twisters book?

Not-so-silly Sausage by Stella Gurney and Liz Million
ISBN 0 237 52875 4

Nick's Birthday by Jane Oliver and Silvia Raga
ISBN 0 237 52896 7

Out Went Sam by Nick Turpin and Barbara Nascimbeni
ISBN 0 237 52894 0

Yummy Scrummy by Paul Harrison and Belinda Worsley
ISBN 0 237 52876 2

Squelch! by Kay Woodward and Stefania Colnaghi
ISBN 0 237 52895 9

Sally Sails the Seas by Stella Gurney and Belinda Worsley
ISBN 0 237 52893 2

Billy on the Ball by Paul Harrison and Silvia Raga
ISBN 0 237 52926 2

Countdown by Kay Woodward and Ofra Amit
ISBN 0 237 52927 0

One Wet Welly by Gill Matthews and Belinda Worsley
ISBN 0 237 52928 9

Sand Dragon by Su Swallow and Silvia Raga
ISBN 0 237 52929 7

Cave-baby and the Mammoth by Vivian French and Lisa Williams
ISBN 0 237 52931 9

Albert Liked Ladders by Su Swallow and Barbara Nascimbeni
ISBN 0 237 52930 0